Acknowledgements

It is with enormous gratitude that we thank each of the women we highlight within this book and beyond for participating in the creation of this text. Not only have they dedicated their time during the crisis to helping others, but they have also dedicated time to us in the creation of this book.

Sheroes of COVID-19

Women leading in the crisis

Co-Authored by	Co-Authored by	Illustrated by
Priya Shah	**Rehmah Kasule**	**Nandi L. Fernandez**

Edited by

Amy Meginnes & Drew Edwards

Pangea Publishing

Foreword

This is a wonderful book that tells us that even in times that are difficult, scary and sad, there are many good people who are helping other people... helping them get well, helping them to learn, helping them to be safe. The Unwelcome Stranger, whom we call COVID or coronavirus, is a virus we cannot see that came into our lives and the lives of people everywhere in the world. This virus made people sick, forced us to stay in our homes to keep from getting sick, and kept children from going to school. Many people lost their jobs and they had to depend on others for food, medicine, and other necessities for themselves and their families.

This book is written by two amazing women who are using their voices to inspire girls and women around the world. The inspiring book tells us about good people who have been helping others during the crisis. It is called "Sheroes" because it is about heroic women and girls who are leading by example. Sometimes women are not taken seriously; sometimes their lives are very difficult.

I was an Ambassador for Women, and I traveled all over the world and saw how hard life was for so many women, but I also saw what extraordinary leaders they were. They were courageous, caring, strong, and compassionate. When they saw a problem, they did not throw up their hands and say, "Why is this happening?"

Instead, they asked, "What can I do to make things better?" They inspired me as I know you will be inspired by the sheroes you are about to meet.

Everyone can be a leader because everyone can help in some way - even in a scary time like this. I am sure these amazing women leaders will inspire you, because when women lead, positive changes happen. You too can be like them. I live in the United States and I know young people who are making face masks; others who are helping to bring groceries to older people in their neighborhood, and still others who are creating fun programs for children to watch on their tablets. It is not important what you do or where you live, so much as it matters that you care and want to help others. That way you can change this scary and difficult time into a better time. Each of these sheroes knows the happiest people in the world are those who care for others and try to help them. A great lesson for life is to know that in giving, we receive. And always remember, never to walk alone; lift another girl as you go.

We are stronger together.

Melanne Verveer
US Ambassador for Global Women's issues (2009-13)
Executive Director, Georgetown Institute for Women, Peace and Security

About the COVID-19 Pandemic

The COVID-19 or the 'coronavirus' pandemic began in December of 2019. The virus has quickly spread from country to country causing danger and spreading fear around the world.

United Kingdom

Canada

United States of America

Ecuador

Peru

People around the world are rising to the challenge. Globally, women make up 70 percent of frontline workers. From healthcare, to social workers, to CEO's, to government leaders, to teachers, to mothers, women are sparking acts of good both big and small and making a difference.

These are the Sheroes of COVID-19.

China

India

United Arab Emirates

Ethiopia

Uganda

anda

Malawi

New Zealand

So much has changed since the arrival
of The Unwelcome Stranger.

My cousin Kato has come to stay. His
parents work at the hospital. I love
spending time with him, but I miss my
school friends. I do not know when
things will be normal again.

"Faith, my dear, what is bothering you?"

"We have been at home for so long, I want to know what is going on out there."

3

"You are not alone. At moments like this, I especially miss your Grandmother. One thing that I learned from her is how important it is to always be looking for the good around us.

Go get your sisters and your cousin - I want to show you something."

4

"In these uncertain times, we have only seen the inside of our home. However, much good is happening all around the world. Knowing that helps us stay positive even during scary times.

When I see something good, I save it for moments like these. I want to share with you some brave stories from this crisis, many of them are of women like you, Faith.

For me, opening this box is like turning on a light.

Let's look together..."

"Many people have become sick with the virus since the outbreak began.

Healthcare workers have done extraordinary things to protect and treat people who are sick," Grandfather said.

7

"Wow! When an ambulance didn't come, Nurse Doris Okudinia in Uganda pushed a patient five kilometers in a wheelchair from her clinic to a hospital! She must have been tired, but kept going!"

Nurse Walks 5KM

"That reminds me of Miss Natalia's job. She is a midwife who is always willing to help the many women in our village give birth to healthy babies," I said.

"That's right. All healthcare workers have shown bravery and strength. Ms. Natalia has been working without a break for months since the crisis started."

"Look - this woman is working to stop the virus!" my sister Zia said. "She's using science to prevent more people from getting sick."

"Yes, there are teams of scientists around the world working to develop a vaccine to help stop the spread of COVID-19."

"Doctors, nurses, and hospital staff have been heroic in how they are serving others."

11

In China, Li Lianglang is a nurse who volunteered to travel to Wuhan, where the outbreak started, to treat people. She and her team performed more than 34 difficult surgeries!"

Healthcare Sheroes

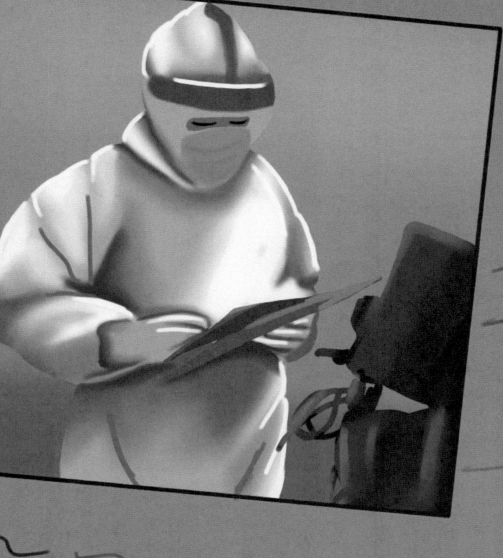

"I feel bad. Doctors are in danger, and I was just feeling sad because I couldn't go outside."

Grandfather put his arm around me. "Our day-to-day activities are different and that can make us sad or angry. It's okay to feel this way."

13

Zia held up a clipping, "lots of people are feeling that way too, Faith. In Chicago, Naimah Thomas is an art therapist who uses art to help kids with their emotions. Her work supports positive mental health during the pandemic. That's health that's not just in your body, but your thoughts and feelings too."`

"This woman, Katz Kiely, from the United Kingdom launched an online service for healthcare workers to request personal protective equipment (PPE) such as masks and goggles. They need those things to stay safe while treating patients."

Helping those who heal

"It can be very hard. A medical student, Sara Lederman, who is just 30 years old, created a babysitting and errand service to help those families."

"Artists and musicians step up to inspire us in moments of fear and despair. Amanda Gorman is only 22 years old, her poetry has inspired people around the world to find light in the darkness of this time."

"There are many ways we can keep our mental health strong. Looking for positive stories together is one. Learning is another, but right now 9 out of 10 children around the world are at home and out of school. That makes learning harder."

"But not impossible! Sajida Shroff in the United Arab Emirates has created a homeschool curriculum for children to learn to read at home with what they have around them."

In Ecuador, the Minister of Education, Monserrat Creamer, has focused learning on emotional well-being and life skills. Students do readings and activities at home related to daily life, and keep them in a portfolio for when they can return to school.

20

"This is so cool! 'Rita Marquez from Chicago teaches children how to create art at home during the lockdown with only the things around them, like coffee grinds!'

We should make art too! Grandfather, we can make a collage of these stories for everyone to see!"

21

"Listen! Right now, it's Jody Unterrheiner and her team on the radio! They do a daily program in Uganda to share knowledge even without phones or tablets. That keeps us learning too!"

"Very good, Faith! Now you are really practicing seeing and hearing the good all around you! Grandmother would be proud."

I felt happy. "I want to be a leader when I am older!"

Grandfather smiled, "In moments of crisis, true leaders rise to guide us. It is not a matter of age, but of action. Leaders give us hope when we are scared and clarity when we are confused. They wake up every day to serve and model how to move forward."

"Wow - just like this...The Minister of Health of Ethiopia, Lia Tadesse, took early action to protect her country which now has one of the lowest rates of infection.

They imposed strict passenger screening at the airport and performed at-home screenings in over 11 million households."

24

Leaders around the world have had to make tough decisions. New Zealand has been celebrated for how they have handled COVID-19. Prime Minister Jacinda Ardern put the nation on strict lockdown earlier than other countries and stayed in communication to help people stay calm and stick to the plan.

Lockdown in our village means most of the shops are closed and that makes earning money difficult," said Zia.

"That is very true, Zia. Leaders, like Toni Alva, the Minister of Economy and Finance of Peru, working to address that by helping small businesses to keep the economy running."

"The Mayor of Dayton Ohio, Nan Whaley, created a way to help non-profits and has been making sure that children have access to breakfast and lunch while school is out."

"You do not need a fancy title to lead. There are people who are leading our communities everyday by keeping essential services running.

Like Aishah and Sophia Ahmed, they are students who inspired other young people to collect thousands of goggles to help workers in their community."

Keeping Families Healthy

"Essential means things we cannot li[ve] without, like food a[nd] clean water. Look at these people all helping in different ways to make sure families can stay healthy."

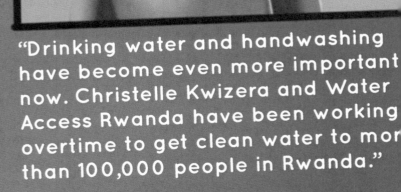

"Drinking water and handwashing have become even more important now. Christelle Kwizera and Water Access Rwanda have been working overtime to get clean water to mor[e] than 100,000 people in Rwanda."

"A woman in Nevada, Jayde Powell, started delivering food to people who can't leave their home. The idea was named Shopping Angels and spread to Canada and Australia. Now, there are more than 6,000 volunteers!"

"People are using their talents to help their communities. Dianna Wara is a baker from the Midwest United States. She bakes fresh bread for her neighbors everyday!"

"Essential as in safety too, right? Grandfather,
I heard someone say that it is not always safe
to be at home. I don't understand."

"Yes, Faith, unfortunately tho
is true. Sometimes the wa
people talk or act in the
homes can be dangerou:
There are many brave peopl
who are working to hel
especially now that w
must stay indoors t
prevent spreadin
COVID-19.

"Elsa Marie D'Silva launched SafeCity, a platform that allows anonymous reporting when something dangerous happens so that community leaders and authorities can take action."

"In Malawi, Patricia Njawili, is one of the police officers who has responded to keep families safe from offenders."

32

Part of protecting people is preventing differences, like religion, from dividing us. Saumya Aggarwal made a game 'Small Acts for Peace' for young people in India to understand how what we say matters and why it's important to work together."

33

"In Canada, Dr. Bonnie Henry has inspired millions and saved lives with communication and clear guidance to 'be kind, be calm, and be safe'."

"Getting accurate information is also important right now. In the United States, WUSA9 reporter-anchor, Delia Gonçalves, has been helping people understand what is happening so that they can make safe decisions," Grandpa said.

"Children, I hope you can start to see that, 'the night sky is never lit by one bright star, it is lit by the billions of stars that come together.' We are stronger when we work together."

"Many people around the world are finding ways to show that they are grateful for all the brave things people are doing during this crisis."

"No Grandfather, that is for us. I think everyone should
know about these brave women, and I have an idea."

38

Even in the darkest of moments, light is always near us. We just have to look for it. Looking for the light is the first step in becoming it.

We are stronger together

List of Sheroes

in order of appearance

Doris Okudinia	Uganda
Li Liangliang	China
Katz Kiely	United Kingdom
Sara Lederman	United States of America
Naimah Thomas	United States of America
Amanda Gorman	United States of America
Sajida Shroff	United Arab Emirates
Monserrat Creamer	Ecuador
Rita Marquez	United States of America
Jody Unterrheiner	Uganda
Lia Tadesse	Ethiopia
Jacinda Ardern	New Zealand
Toni Alva	Peru
Nan Whaley	United States of America
Aishah & Sophia Ahmed	United States of America
Christelle Kwizera	Rwanda
Jayde Powell	United States of America
Dianna Wara	United States of America
Elsa Marie D'Silva	India
Patricia Njawili	Malawi
Saumya Aggarwal	India
Delia Gonçalves	United States of America
Dr. Bonnie Henry	Canada

Comprehension Questions

Although crises bring challenges, there are forms of positivity that always surrounds us - in our environment, in ourselves, and in others. We call this the simple good. We praise Sheroes because they always carry the simple good and bring light to those around them.
Pull out a sheet of paper and find a quiet space to answer the following questions:

1. Who is the 'Unwelcome Stranger'?

2. What is a 'shero?

3. What are the character qualities of a shero?

4. What countries did these sheroes make an impact in? Do you know anyone from these countries?

5. Which shero's story were you inspired by? What was their simple good?

6. Share an example of a shero in your own community. What are they doing? Who does it help?

Activities

Sheroes are courageous, compassionate, kind, and thoughtful. It's not just women or famous leaders that can do something to respond to COVID-19, everyone can. It begins with seeing these traits in ourselves, but also seeing them in others. Celebrate the "sheroes" you see around you and share their stories with others!

Stop & Think

Who are the sheroes in your own community? Take a moment to reflect on how you can also make an impact on your community. What are 3 forms of positivity that already live within you? How do you think the above traits could impact someone else?

Do

Pick one of your characteristics and use it to serve others around you.

Reflect and Share

What did you learn? Share your project with others so they can do the same in their own community. Upload a photo of your service and tell us how it made a difference at #StrongerTogether.

Pangea Educational Development is a 501(c)3 non-profit organization registered in the USA and Uganda. The organization's mission is to empower individuals and communities to fulfill their own purpose and potential by fostering cultures of literacy. It accomplishes this through improving early grade literacy instruction, increasing book access, and changing the narrative in literature by increasing representation.

Our Partners

CEDA International is a 501(c)3 non profit registered in USA and Uganda focusing on girls education, youth and gender empowerment, workforce and enterprise development, and financial inclusion for people at the bottom of the pyramid. The organization aims at creating new generations of transformational women leaders and entrepreneurs who are economically independent, socially responsible and politically active.

The Simple Good is a 501(c)3 non-profit organization whose mission is to connect the meaning of good from around the world to empower youth to become positive activists through art and discussion. Through mindfulness and Social Emotional Learning (SEL) based art programming and public art projects, our mission is to transcend the message that no matter where you go in the world, good means the same to all of us and that is what connects us as human beings.

Made in the USA
Monee, IL
24 September 2020

"So important. So relatable. So human. Sheroes of COVID-19 is an inspiration to our families in a time when we need just that. This is a great learning opportunity for people as young as 4 and old as 104. It is a leadership book, a geography book, a hopeful book, and an understanding book."
— Geraldine Laybourne, first President of Nickelodeon and advocate for children and women

"This special book shows how women are leading during the COVID-19 pandemic. No matter who you are or where you come from, you can make life better for your community. Just look around you, then take initiative to make things better. And keep reading and encourage others to do the same!"
— Dr. Ronald F. Ferguson, Harvard University Professor and Founder, The Basics

"Everyone can be a leader because everyone can help in some way—even in a scary time like this. I am sure these amazing women leaders will inspire you, because when women lead, positive changes happen."
—Melanne Verveer, Executive Director, Georgetown Institute for Women, Peace and Security and Former U.S. Ambassador for Global Women's Issues

Pangea
Publishing

$14.99
ISBN 978-1-7356812-0-7
51499>

9 781735 681207